BOOK REVIEWS

In the realm of poetry, there exists a subgenre that delves into the depths of human emotion, exploring the raw and often tumultuous experiences that color our lives. Kleo's "The Loss of Fire" is a poignant collection of angst-ridden verses that plumbs the depths of the struggles of the human spirit.

Kleo's poems are not for the faint of heart. They are stark, unflinching portrayals of the pain that can consume us, laid bare with a vulnerability that is both unsettling and deeply moving. Yet, amidst the darkness, there are glimmers of hope and delicate threads of resilience that weave their way through the verses. Kleo's language, while often melancholic, is infused with a haunting beauty that captures the essence of human longing.

In a world that often strives to conceal its vulnerabilities, "The Loss of Fire" stands as a courageous act of self-expression. Kleo's poems are a testament to the enduring power of poetry to confront the darkest corners of the human heart and, in doing so, offer a glimmer of solace and understanding.

— Jon West- Bey

Jon West-Bey is a curator, museologist, and museum consultant based in Washington, DC. He is a Lecturer in the Master of Arts in Museum Studies program at the Krieger School of Arts & Sciences at Johns Hopkins University. He is also the Founder and former Executive Director of the American Poetry Museum in Washington, DC.

The Loss of Fire" by Kleo is a truly captivating literary masterpiece. Kleo's writing skillfully immerses readers in a mesmerizing world, almost like watching a short film. Her ability to take you on an emotional journey, allowing you to share in her highs and lows, while witnessing her triumphs and personal growth, is remarkable. I eagerly anticipate more literary works from this talented author in the future.

— Lyrical Soul, fellow poet and editor

To order additional copies of this book, contact:
Xlibris
844-714-8691
www.Xlibris.com
Orders@Xlibris.com

ISBN: Softcover   979-8-3694-1009-7
        EBook   979-8-3694-1010-3

Library of Congress Control Number: 2023920638

Print information available on the last page

Rev. date: 11/29/2023

CONTENTS

PERSONAL NARRATIVES OF MY ANXIETY
[AND OTHER ISSUES I HAVE]   45

GROWING PAINS [AND IDENTITY FORMATION]

Growing Pain

Family always said I would have growing pains
But since my legs never got to stretching past
5'4, I figured that didn't apply to me
Until I felt it in my gums

The reality of adulthood approached me and I
was confused, baffled
How dare time tell me I was entitled to
experiencing pain

It started slow
It would wiggle and wobble and then get pulled
I always pulled it
Never wanted anyone else to pull it because it
would cause me pain
Like my dad did when he left
So I caused it myself

As one left another grew and as my heart broke
itself, it healed in different ways
Molded itself into new shapes
I'm pretty sure it doesn't hold it's same shape
That nice neat red heart that beats at a perfect
rhythm
well, mines just bleeds

My two front teeth were the worst, leaving a
gaping space only to be filled with the biggest
pieces of bone I've seen
They got made fun of and so did my skin and
bones of a body

But the worst pain was the unexpected
just when I thought the growth was over
that the final product was good
Wisdom hit me like a brick to the jaw and never
stopped
The throbbing pain fought through my gums so
hard they pierced the surface
and reminded me of the last time I grew
Painfully
Making me beg for relief
For some remedy
For some way to suddenly fix me
But I had nothing
So I prayed for surgical procedures to be done
for metal as cold as my appearance to make its
way into my mouth
And as I wait for the laughing gas to kick in
I wondered about you
Did you ever imagine what it felt like to wake up
to me in the morning
To feel how soft my wild mane was as it filled
your pillow with perfumes
Forget it, just pull the damn tooth

Growing Pain's by Indigo Quashie

People Who Hurt
People, Hurt Me

You will ask about my scars one day
And the only thing I can muster up to tell you
Is that it happened a long time ago?
It's barely a mark now
Only a simple scratch
Because acknowledging it
Also highlights the idea that I'm vulnerable
enough to show it
Vulnerable enough to write it out
And present it to you for evaluation
the grade?
If you're even willing to stay after my story
My book
My journal
I don't want to trust anyone else with my scars
Because as soon as I mention them you make fake
promises to fix them
Acknowledge you would never leave a scar like
that
You just left something worse
A new wound

Life with Skinny Girl's Bifocals

Age 12: They said: "You're too skinny"
Fearful of wearing t-shirts, the sleeves on my
extra-small Aeropostale are pulled to threads
I always made sure I got an extra small so that
maybe my body could have some shape
Maybe my **32 A's** would manage to look like B's
for a day if I just did the buttons like this
Covering my wrists because the bones presence is
more apparent than the skin
I carried **99 lbs.** of shy, raging insecurity while **115
lbs.** of what girls should be, mocked me
I was not what a Black woman should be

Age: 15 they said: "Why don't you just eat more?"
Black women are the cream of the crop
Born as curvaceous beings
And I
Born with twigs for legs and ant hills for breasts
Peanut Butter
Cornbread and my personal favorite: collard greens
We're my fake friends
With all the promises they hold for everyone else
to me they couldn't keep
So no, I'm sorry but my family isn't the
stereotypical Black one you see on TV
Mama raised me with grilled fish and spinach
For breakfast, Oatmeal and eggs greeted me
I liked my fruits and veggies too but my bones
lacked meat

Age 16: "Welcome to Instagram; would you like
to allow notifications?"
Posting pictures from the face up so boys won't
see how I'm not developing like my friends are
Holding up the peace sign to avoid snapping the fact
that my body holds more constellations than clear skin
Removing smiles from selfies so my two front
teeth aren't the stars of the show

Soon enough I found myself removing my smile
from everyday interaction

Eye contact becomes less frequent with human
interaction and more focused on the notifications
from a screen
Click
I like that
Tap to the popular page
Why am I not beautiful enough?
Scroll
Scroll
Scroll
Relationship
Funny joke
Relationship
tbh
People who didn't invite me to their birthday
dinner, but were friends in class and they ask me
for all the answers
Slowly pictures gave the conclusion that the world
offered beautiful women and none of them were me

Age 19:
We've come a long way you and me
And guess what
ya still skinny
That **99lbs** turned into **125**
Freshman 15 ain't got nothing on me and I low-
key like it
Yeah my cheeks have filled, my thighs rub, and I
got a lil sum in the back
Inside I'm not the same girl who looks for love in
a tbh on snapchat
When the skinny girl disappeared so did her needs
Insecurities shrunk and packed and placed in
boxes only accessible through poetry that work
daily to unpack a smile

People Watching

I watch everyone find love
I watch as the sparks fly and cannons boom
I observe as the butterflies imply stuttering
phrases and soft giggles that result in smiles wide
like night sky
I go out to lunch and glance at first dates
A little careful with how you chew
Hoping conversation doesn't end or never running
out of conversation because this
is the one
I peep holding hands for the first time
Leaving in the morning and hoping to avoid too
much noise as you
Dammit
Bump something and it sounds as loud as
wedding bells

I observe serious talks that lead to care being
portrayed through anger
I hear the wrong thing
I watch the ending
And the beginning of coming back together
because what we have is too special to let
go of …
We all have centers love rests at mine
It's bed is made up nice waiting to be laid in
But no one ever does they're afraid the springs
will rust, the water bed will pop
which leaves me watching hearing
Craving for a taste but being left empty

Self-Love

I loved the way that you loved me
The way that you called me beautiful upon approach
That was the first time I've ever heard it and it
sounded as foreign as the fruit we can never bring
back from trips my dreams took
You used to buy me gifts
Ones that really mattered and I would do the
same for you as a first love it was only right that
we gave each other everything, right?
Talked about imaginary marriages with kids from
clouds and houses made of stars but as time went
on we knew we couldn't travel that far
How you looked at me when I walked in the
room
You would steal glances at me
sometimes smile and I would pretend I didn't see
you and act like we were strangers

Because deep down I loved that shit
lived for it from all the days I used to sit in bed
alone and watch rom coms produced by fake love
studios and directed by infatuation
You made me understand dedication
I used to miss things for you, but in the missing
of banquets and lunch dates and countless
opportunities of escaping you
You taught me to
Believe in myself
Over think
Express myself
Yell
Create art

Miscommunicate
Feel like absolute shit without a purpose

See my point ?
You used to write me poems
About how I should be yours and how the magic
we created out of pure raw energy
But as your poetry faded into simple letters
I wrote more poems for him about how he
changed everything
About how special he was
About how I truly felt love even though, it wasn't for us
He never wrote me any poems
Never gave me any gifts
All of you wrapped up excuses and tied them
with the bows of my insecurities to make the
package look pretty
I loved all of you
I loved the way you loved me
I loved you until I had nothing left to give
'Til it damn near destroyed me
'Til hate became your emotion
And until memories wore thin like an over washed
shirt in my mind
Rinse cycle repeat
So I hid myself In a cocoon wrapped tight
Breaking promises I made led me to all of you
So now, I sew those promises into wings
And as I leave your nest and stumble to fly
I realize
I loved your love because that is how I always
wanted to love me.

Another Prompted Poem for Uncle Rodney

Prompt: A lost item from that items perspective

I just want to apologize
I want to start with this
I'll never forgive myself for my lack of responsibility
Who knew at 16 I could still lose things
That I could force materials to hold memory
That's what I did to you
I think God knew I had to let you go
I couldn't keep something so concrete too close to
the abstract of what you were
I know what you weren't
You weren't him
So I'm sorry .. I'm sorry I misplaced you in a place
I still don't know
Feel free to yell or scream or throw yourself at me
It's fine ... what do you think ?

How could you ?
I loved the feeling of you more than anything
I wrapped myself around you tightened the grip
hoping you would never let go
But you did
I know you didn't mean it
Honestly, it was a casual day
One moment I was a part of you and the next ..
well I can't really remember

He meant it though
He pulled the grip on the trigger and let go for me,
I never knew why
Nobody else did either
Not the street lamp
The grocer
The parking lot
My son
The mother of my child
I want you to know I thought about you all of you

I thought about that time you first got me
You said mommy would like me because I was blue
That is her favorite
But now that you look back, it was kind of green too
Just like you
A compromise
I liked me because I represented so much for you
He brought you to get me
I never thought you would lose him
I'm sorry you only grew to love me because of that
I wanted to mean so much to you but since we're here
I held so much power
Brought back so many tears

Matter of fact
I meant too much to you
That's why you had to lose me
No no, it's okay
It's better that way
You see, I need you to remember these times
I need you to remember the hugs
The early mornings and late nights
The times where you told me don't ever sleep
with the covers over your face because there's not
enough air under there
There wasn't enough air in the room when you lost me
Wasn't enough air when you saw my face on the news
The blue and red lights that covered your senses
with anxiety and dread

I want you to know It can't be all about me
It's too selfish of me
I know you didn't mean it
Where you left me is where i'll always be
Tucked away in a crevice of your heart
I hope you'll never forget about me
I know you'll never forgive yourself
That's why out of all things you chose the
turquoise heart surrounded by a ring

Terrible Luck [and Taste] With Men

I did it all right this time
I think
Checked all the boxes
Was careful with everything I did
Yet and still
I remain unsatisfied
Remain full of unanswered questions
I keep failing this test
this exam
this pop quiz
Whatever the hell you're giving me
So I find my way back to the books
Out of isolation
It's easier to keep learning
than to actually practice
It's easier to reject opinion over fact
and the fact is
The fact doesn't matter
The fact is
I don't know anything.

Co-star

Co-star reads me for filth everyday
talking about "find comfort in the idea that
nothing lasts forever"
and of course, I think of you
Think of the way I still notice your presence
whenever you enter a room
or the way that we both ignore each other as If
we're two blind mice in search of the third
but nobody is ignoring each other as strongly as
we do
No one is mentally slapping themselves 1,000
times and contemplating using various unhealthy
coping mechanisms like I am
or are you ?
I guess we'll never know
but I'm going to assume the answer is no
Because you know
and I know
That I'm always the last thing reminiscing around
the frontal lobe
But one day I hope to be

Anyways,
back to Co-star and using computer algorithms to
say general statements and apply them to my life
Asking me how I undermine myself

And I think of how disrespect rolls off the tongue
or more so the eyes of me when I reminisce on
how we used to be
How we used to stay up late and always regret it
in the morning
How we used to be so comfortable we forgot we
weren't alone
How we lied to each other about what we wanted
Well I didn't
Either way
I'm supposed to be practicing forgiveness
but that isn't working so well

So instead
I think of endless letters I could write
Words I could say
Almost to the point of being apologetic
and it's almost as if the pain was the first thing I forgot
because it isn't my fault
Isn't my fault that you called it quits before we
gave it a chance
And as an attempt to create the change I wanted
to see ...
I changed nothing
Stuck around for the repetitive bullshit
and wouldn't let the pain be the first thing I forgot
because I got to the point where I thought I deserved it
Deserved love that hurt
Deserved some sort of karma
But whose karma am I getting for loving vulnerably
To the point of insanity
To the point of anxiety
At least with my Co-star, I can see when karma is
coming.

Avow to Last Summer (2019)

This is dedicated to the last summer
For it to be different
For it to feel like something new
For it to not be boring
Maybe a little scary
Maybe a litter summer like
and to over all remind me that summer days Are
fleeting with the rest of our days

And it was
Soooo different
from top to bottom
Filled with cumulonimbus clouds
Laughter
and sometimes tears
But never for long
Only so that I could see my reflection in the
mirror cleared
Only so that I could learn a lesson
or 12
or the same one 12 times
Happens so much now these days I can't tell
but I'm learning to

I put on a new skin
got tired of trying to fit in others
It got too hot
Too hot for societal standards
Too hot for me go to and from work everyday
without water
So I started appreciating it more

I changed my hair 5 times
and didn't care if anyone noticed
because I did
And I loved
Each
And
Every
One
Even made a vow to grow it out for now
so we'll see how long that lasts

Until

Always considered myself a lover of nature
Until birds chirp at 6 am with rude awakenings
and morning reports
Shitting on my hand unconsciously
and secretly haunting me in my nightmares
The worst are the crows
Black as midnight with a screeching noise for a voice
But that's not the point

Always considered myself incapable of fear when
it comes to bugs
But bees sting
and leave a memory that is a bit more frightening
Mosquitos suck and get as greedy as can be
and honestly
I think mosquitos should replace both the birds
and the bees

I mean they create constant paranoia
and the last time I can recall not being paranoid
about love is when I didn't expect it
Because nobody told me I had to ever be scared
of birds or bees
until I got stung
And nobody taught me how to treat it

The One in the Huffington Post

To be Black is to be the warmth of the brightest of
sun rays
To feel Black is the greatest challenge
To feel the culture
The stories of countless tragedies and joys
It's all consuming
So listen to my story of how I felt Black
A story I can't take back
that I would never want to change

Don't touch my hair
It's my crown, my heritage
What if I took your history and played with it like a
toy ?
I knew I was Black the moment my classmates
wouldn't stop asking about my hair
How do you get it like that ?
Why don't you just straighten it ?
You mean you've never had a relaxer ?

No Becky
Instead after I get home from school I gotta do my
homework immediately
take a shower and wet my mane because my
momma is about to take a comb and a brush
some gel
and pink stuff from a bottle
and make it do with what it do
Make it braids with butterfly barrettes at the end
Make it puffs that start off small but are bigger
than volleyballs at the end of the school day
Or my favorite when she takes the time to twist all
of my curls

Either way that's 1.5 hours of my day that I could
never explain
Filled with laughs and tears
Filled with stories that I carry on my head and in
my heart

And that's what makes me Black
When I would sit in the white salons and have
two blow dryers on my head
Fighting back tears because getting a relaxer
would be so much easier
So much easier to try to tame myself to fit into
Becky's standards
But momma wouldn't stand for that

Do you know the history of black hair ?
Kept under scarves and caps because the white
folks ain't want to see it
Putting rice in the braids to make sure there wasn't
a chance at starvation
Inventing creamy crack so I can get a job that still
makes me break my back five times over for five
times less than Becky
I know y'all hear me
I know you know that pain
The pain of wanting to fit in
And sadly for a moment wish not to be Black
But I would hate to not be Black
I would never go back
And most importantly I would never do that
creamy crack

The Pain of Eve

There is no warning
No trigger either
Just a random moment
When all of a sudden
you're getting repeatedly kicked in the stomach
Some kicks more aggressive than others
Some reach the ribs
and others head for the opposite direction
Hurry
Hurry
How do I stop it?
The attack on Eve
of Eve maybe
Will it work with a simple unclasp ?
How about an unbutton ?
Let's try untying ..

And now I'm a mess on the floor
Naked of hoop earrings
and a combination of mascara and lipgloss
That covered up
the pain of Eve

The pain in everything
as I search for the nearest bottle of orange or blue pills
and swallow four with a swiftness because two
stopped working after I had to stay home all day
from 7th grade cramps

There is ..
No release
No fast remedy
Except to put on a smile and excuse yourself
Quietly
As I crave the moment
Where it's just me
A heating pack
No jeans
Possibly camomile tea
No kicking
Definitely chocolate
All as I battle the monthly beating from Eve

BIRDS OR BEES

I don't even remember the talk honestly
Mainly because ignorance was still bliss
Mainly because I loved my rose tinted glasses
but I'm assuming after that day
Roses started to wilt like Beauty and the Beast
and I started to become curious about the birds
and the bees

Curious about the ways that I could capture
intimacy in a jar and keep it there
Hold it captive
Making sure its light never dimmed
but it always does
Even if I poke holes for air
It's not enough
And freedom from my intimacy is always better
Restrictions are ideal
Only on your time and not mine
You and I only get to feel like we on the days that
you like

Who the hell asked for my opinion anyways?
So am I the bird or the bee?
Irritating as hell with beaded eyes but beautiful wings
or am I dead but satisfied and purposeless after one
sting ?

Aesthetically pleasing myself.

I do it all for me
The big hoop earrings
The glitter on my legs
The confidence in my walk
just to feel good
Know I'm good
Feel like a woman
even though 21 barely scratches the surface
I'll try anyways
to be grown
Oh I have so much to learn
and who will help me?
Just the mistakes I make along the way
Over
and over again
But they make my poems aesthetically pleasing
So It's okay

The Art of Being Missed

So what time is a good time for me to double text
you ??
You still haven't seen the one from yesterday
but I really want to tell you this one joke
I promise it will make you laugh
Actually
Maybe I should just call
He always told me to do that because
"I'm not on my phone a lot and I hate to text"
Whether it's the truth or an excuse it doesn't affect
what I do next
I'll wait a few rings and then hang up to avoid rejection
Because the last time I called you were unavailable
and I found it symbolic for our connection

Here I go moving too fast
Connection ?
Double texting?
Don't you know how to slow down and just let
shit be ?
Mama says you should understand the art of
being missed
You have mastered it and well me
I'm still waiting for a text back
Sent it this morning and made myself busy so I
would be excited for when I finally heard back.
Because I always hear back

Just not in the time frame that I would like
Checking my phone every fifteen minutes and
Sike !
You played yourself
Again
I keep waiting on the day that I win
That someone is searching their phone for me
Waiting this long it might be this way for the rest
of history
Me always turning into predator instead of prey
Because I know what I want but others never see
it that way
"You make it too easy, you gave him all he wanted
this early and you expected him to stay"
Yes

With everything in me I wish I could confidently
say yes
But you and I both know the maturity of a man
determines everything
And I have little patience to wait on a text back
But in the past I've had all this patience with
getting treated like trash
So maybe I will practice being missed
Then when I shoot I might score leaving him with
something to reminisce

Self Fear

There are times
When I just…
No matter how hard I try
I just feel like the darkest version of the night
Like the things that go bump in it
The things that I fear I am
The monsters I run from are internalized instead
And they don't die
don't rest
or propose leaving
Maybe I've made them a comfortable home
Maybe that's why I can't escape them
No matter how fast I run
They just grow
Until there's nothing left of me
Just my face with a monster of a soul underneath.

All of My Scars

All of my scars never really hurt
Trust me
They aren't as bad as they look
It's more so the quantity that's alarming
The scars that are worrisome
But for me they are only stories

Like for my clumsiness
As I crash into a mailbox
and a garage
and a stop sign
... Okay maybe bikes aren't for me

Like for the embarrassment of adolescence and
mean middle schoolers
Who didn't help me as I tripped and busted my
knee open on cement stairs
Who laughed as I tried to learn to hurdle for the
100th time
.. Okay maybe I should just be more direct with
my foot placement

Well what about the ones now?
I had no idea skin burned so easily
Well my skin specifically
Can you believe that?
Believe that I'm not indestructible?
Because I'm still coming to grips with it

Coming to grips with the fact that it takes years for
scrapes and bruises to heal

Yet I keep getting them
Keep reminding myself that boys are stupid as
I trip over them
You clumsy b**ch

Whoa
Don't call yourself that

If we're placing blame for scars let's blame gravity
or weight
As I crash into the pool innocently
How could you have known I'd forgotten how to
swim?
That I would scrape my leg in three places

Well I guess for every healed scar there are three
more that come to replace it
For every new year of birth there is a new bruise
to show you can't escape it
but you can ice the pain
Elevate the knees
and place a heat pad on the back
Apply ointment
and clean with peroxide because alcohol burns
Both kinds
Just feels like it creates more scars
I'm still talking about both kinds
anyways put a band-aid on it
or wear a brace
do anything to get rid of those scars that are so
conveniently misplaced

IN MY SUBCONSCIOUS

Cut and Cure

I've made a fire before
held the power in my hands
I've seen the spark of orange hues hit my eyes
Felt it punch my soul at the same time
Oh wait, that was you.

I've felt crazy before
I've ripped my heart out just for you to see that it
only beats for you
I've had tears find a familiar place on my face
I've let them make a home there
I've wondered if I should let the car hit me or just
let it be

I've let my rage turn from orange to white
I've watched you burn and felt revenge
I've left the ugly scar that you try to use average
lotion to fix
I've placed a wicked smile on my face to hide the pain
You almost uprooted me because of your lingering
You were the wildfire that almost destroyed my sap
Funny thing is ... I'm an aloe vera plant

A Line..

I don't think you can understand my addiction to
music
I'm as connected to my earphones as an ocean
is to the sand

The Time I Won A Slam Contest

I've rehearsed speaking to you out loud
instead of unconsciously a million times
So now that I have the chance
I'll stand up straight
Make direct eye contact
No.
No eye contact.
This sounds so much better when I'm confident
It looks so much better when I'm not afraid or
distracted or can't get my points across or try to
refrain from screaming ...
So here we go
I
I really
I really don't
I really don't understand
I really don't
don't understand how anyone of my friends can
be friends with you
But
But I'm trying
trying to
But it's one of the hardest concepts I've never
been able to wrap my head around
wrap my heart around
because you hurt me
and not just me
I mean the whole being
I questioned throwing my whole self away
I almost hated the actions I took and the words
that escaped my mouth
but then .... I realized

you
you didn't do
you didn't do anything to them
not a damn thing
you lied in my face but not theirs
you broke my heart, but they only watched only
interpreted
offered advice but still told me to stay away
also told me that love was rare
but that shit isn't rare enough if *you* keep fucking
finding it
You made love to me
You loved me
You loved
the feeling
The feeling that I-
The feeling of comfort and conformation
I brought you
At least I thought so
know so
I wish I could make them feel it but at the same
time
At the same time
At the same damn time
I'm selfish
with your love and my friends
But your love doesn't exists so I just want all my
fucking friends
and I mean all of them
acquaintances and all
back.

Flag on the Play

Red flags wave in the sky like cranes
and every time I look up they get closer and closer
I pray harder and harder that they are wrong
and for a moment they look white
and I feel safe
safe from the attack of the peanut gallery
throwing everything at me that they got
torturing my mental with the idea that you are just as
bad as the others and I should've seen this coming
I wouldn't ask so many times if I didn't feel like
you were ready
or you truly didn't want me
or just me but more
many
multiple
and it makes me want to fucking scream

but instead I try and talk with my heart as my
tongue and you still shoot me down guns blazing
and my heart plunges into my stomach as I feel
like the largest failure
like I'm making you lose
and maybe it's better if it's not just me
if it's not me at all
as I wait for a reply and drown in the tears I
can't cry

Fears of the Korprate World and Double Consciousness

What do you tell a Black woman about being
successful ?
You tell her go to school
Pay attention in class
Come home and do your homework
Love and happiness come last
You tell her to smile
Sit up straight
Be a people pleaser

The days of pleasing the master are never over
The current system is just a deceiver
Tell the Black woman that she's at the bottom
so her boot straps are long and skinny
Brittle enough to break upon the first pull
but that doesn't matter
Excuses aren't tolerated

Tell her that it's okay if your boss uses micro
aggressions to start conversations

Sure it won't lead to a raise in minimum wage
Only pure frustration and subdued rage
Caution, don't let the Black woman out the cage
can't let her be untamed
even down to the simplest things like the mane
tell her to press
stress
and apply heat in the form of chemical filled
creams

Just to look like those white girls who woke up like that
Tell her to be a people pleaser to the man
and a fake friend to the woman
Be an advocate for everyone Black
but still an individual
Drowned by deadlines to create content
produce results
Close the deal
As long as she's at 9-5 she's not allowed to feel
You'll be fine as long as you apply enough
makeup to resemble a poker face
Oh and also why I have you here
Know you'll make less than everyone here
Also don't be mad when you hear that one
coworker use racial slurs
We don't care that they're possibly racist
they bring in good numbers
Don't expect to actually catch a break
We're working you until you realize your worth
and eventually quit
Oh and last but not least
Don't come in here angry
You know the stereotypes are real
and you scare us
So Black woman
I hope you heed my warning
hear my truth
Because a Black woman can only be herself
between the hours 5-9 and never from 9-5

Thank you Langston (Inspired by Langston Hughes Mother to Son)

Crystal stairs and golden rails
With a pretty woman standing behind the veil
She wears diamonds and pearls that droop with
emerald and ruby red seas
Who is she ?
She's a mystery
A tall tale
A myth about a goddess who snatched crowns
until they all melted into one on her crown
With a head held high
Her shadow is 12 feet tall
But what if the crystal staircase is simply glass?
And the golden rails are painted like cheap
jewelry from Claire's?
Just like the ones around her neck
What if she slaughtered for crowns only to result
in them lying powerless upon her head
The mystery
The tall tale
The mythical goddess
is simply just a 12 ft shadow
Life for her ain't been no crystal stair
Because behind the sleek Black dress that
encompasses her energy
there are scars
marks
scab wounds from the crowns she snatched
The power grab took more power than actual
grabbing from the men who once held them

With their swords for tongues and guns for hands
that fire away without consent
There's no telling what's behind that veil

My life ain't been no crystal stair
My staircase has cracks in it if you really want to
inspect
The crystal around my neck is as close as we're
going to get
With no seas of red or green
no veil
There is no alluring factor about me
So I look to the pretty woman with a crystal stair
and golden rails
who hides her scars behind a Black veil
I look to her for guidance but she only ponders
about breaking the beautiful glass staircase

A Prompted Poem: Write about me as a poet not writing ever again

How do I not start this poem as a cliché goodbye?
I guess all goodbyes are cliché
They all fill the tongue with sappy language and
salty tears
With this goodbye, I only have fear
The fear of losing myself
See, another cliché
Let's try this again.
In a totally cheesy cliché poetry way

I met you when I was thirteen
and from the start
I didn't think we would be friends
You weren't cool enough for me
and you just took too much damn time
But on the dark days where letters weren't enough
When songs couldn't hit the sweet spot and I
couldn't hit the notes
You were there
With blank pages ready for ink to be spewed all
over them
You let me paint you
Creative with my thoughts
and dirty with my secrets

The first time I needed you
I was 18

In a year of curiosity, you made sure to ask me if I
was good when nobody else did
You stayed up with me when I couldn't sleep and
you stayed close to me as ink became finger taps
onto a white screen
With the brightness low so my roommate could sleep

I needed you way more that you needed me
way more than the skill needed me because to the
officials of English
I ain't that good
I have no rhyme scheme
There is no rhythm to the syllables here
I don't use big words to make it all confusing and
deep and abstract
I leave it to the pros to do all that

But that isn't enough for you
Is it?
I'm 20 years old
The prime time
The selfish years
The years of my greatest inspiration
I thought I could do us justice, but I just can't get it
Time and time again I want to be good for you
But I can't
It's not me it's you
Wait
Wrong way to say the cliché
It's not you it's me

Without you here I can't even be
But I'm not good enough for you so clearly it's
time for you to leave
Just like everyone else
So take everything with you
Matter of fact how about you lose yourself
don't ever let me find you again because I swear I
won't let you go
You know I hate that this is how we say goodby-

Privacy

It felt like a movie
The type that starts with a girl whose life is in
complete and utter dysfunction

In this scene, I walked the stairs alone
ascending into darkness
When suddenly, I enter a room of rainbow auras
and bright hues
My room
My space
but my window awaits
With the blinds open from the earlier day
They are typically used to let the sun come in and
hug the space but this was different
The sun was gone and all that was left was white
nights with frozen air
But back to the window

There is another room that holds another life
one more eventful than mine
with a boy and a girl who interlock like a Black girls
curls
Two lovers grasp each other for air as they add
and subtract from one another
the boy adds a hand to grip her waist as she
subtracts clothing
and for a moment
I'm in that life
I feel the spark that lights the fire
the wave that crashes on the shore
the way that everything stops

as love is made
as he pulls her as close as she can get without
making her apart of him and absorbing her
completely
and as time stops for them
I am still left here across the way in a different
house
with a different window
who admires privacy
and closes the blinds

If A Tree Falls and no one is A-round

A tree falls
In the woods
On a dark night
And I'm there
The roots scream
The branches beckon
And my mouth is gaping wide
As my tongue realizes it has been sliced from its owner
And the splinters rip through my flesh
And with all the pain of silence
I hear laughter
I hear the mockingbirds sing their song as the
crows fly above me
The vultures begin to descend but find nothing left
to eat
Except my confidence that left with my tongue as
I found comfort in the fallen tree
Covering myself with its leaves
Tangled up in its branches
Feeling the memories as tree sap oozes me Down
memory lane
and it reminds me.
You are the girl who nobody listens to
Your tree makes no sound when it falls in the forest
There is no crash or no boom and with that I light
the fuse
Or don't
Instead like the tree, I disintegrate

As my hard oak rots my hollow shell leaves me
ready for the decay of another day
When my voice isn't there
When no matter how loud
How sweet
How proud
I say this
I am silenced

Playing the MF Game (and not liking "having hoes")

I don't think exhausted is fitting
I'm not drained necessarily
but I am tired
of the games
The antics
The norms
That surround me and you
All of us
It's just ...
The same
Every time
Person meets person
They ring around the roses
Ride the carousel
Meanwhile person three is just waiting in line
For their chance to hop on
Chance to try the ride
See if it's a good fit for them

See if they can make it worthwhile even though
the sensation is consistently temporary
And that's why I'm tired
Tired of sensation not lasting
It's losing its luster
It's shine
Pizazz
And I'm left feeling
Unsatisfied and having no urge
Not a singular one
To play the game of human interest

Burning Sage Until
I Pass Out

It would be a waste of breath for me to express
the fatigue I feel
To put into words how exhausted I am from this space
From trying to please others
From attempting to accept myself
From trying to burn enough sage to get rid of all of
people's negative bs
But here I am
Yet again explaining how exhausted I am
The real question is where can I find energy?
Where can I refuel?

Re-spark a light in my eye that left a long time ago
Find a way to feel like someone actually cares
when the room says the opposite
When it caters to the later
That's why silence is best
My silence is infinite
At least it feels like it
Invisibility becomes me because to you my voice
never mattered anyways
So I stopped using it.

Lies I Told Myself

I fear that people will always forget
that I'll always be unseen
The scary thing is, sometimes I like it that way
but most times,I hate it
Hate how it makes me nervous
That you are only visible to me
and I
Invisible to you
Un-memorable to say the least
And it's the most terrifying thing ever
Because you make me feel seen
But that feeling never lasts long
Almost like a sugar high
I love it while it's there and always notice when
it's gone.
Will you finally notice me when I'm gone?

Self Love

I'm trying to enjoy being alone
to smile in the quiet moments
and enjoy the sky when I don't recognize
anything else.
I'm trying to feel good without the pressure of
constantly pleasuring someone
or feeling nervous when they're away
I always felt that way with you
and it made me question everything
Including myself

I'm trying to love myself
and in weekdays that's pretty easy
on the weekends
with more free time
and more use of whatever is in my cup
I miss having someone to call when I have nothing
on my plate
But something is always on my plate
purposefully

Attempting not to be greedy
I just want to see how far I can stretch myself
How much I can stack before the plate shatters
under pressure

I'm trying to take care of myself
lighting two candles and maybe a bowl to get me
through the day
washing my face twice a day
creating a routine
and sticking to it
fashioning morals
and maybe even a few standards

As the candles run out of wax to burn
I forget my routines
and get seasonal acne as easy as depression
I find the parts I hate, everyone else admires

Transparent Lines

Today I told myself I had morals
Made rules
Wrote them down
Tried to make them neat
But life isn't
And neither are my left handed ink smears
So you can imagine it got a little messy
But
Legible

They weren't gently placed within the margin
Because I wanted to leave room for me to cross
the line
To make mistakes yet still be gentle with myself
A good criteria
A realistic rule
I can promise you I'll try to follow that one a
hundred percent
And as I try to wonder what mistakes i'll make

I already know it will involve a combination of
nerves and lust

Like those tv shows I watch
Combine crossing the line and walking it
Most likely from a combo of smoke and liquid from
the gas that someone always seems to supply
You can rely on me keeping a bottle of wine
So maybe I need to add that rule to the list too
with an asterisk that reads
*Drugs shall only be used Friday - Sunday at 2 am
for the purposes of self enjoyment*
Yet your hand at the small of my back is enjoyable
enough for me
As I brush your lips with mine
Combine it with my bottle of wine
and boom
here I am yet again
crossing the line

In Your Blocks Please

It's as quiet as death
Yet not as threatening
More welcoming than anything
It waits for you
At that line
Waits for you to breathe and shake
Jump and stretch
And maybe even send a quick prayer to whoever
you pray to
For health and legs that move faster than light
and even though we know it's not as possible as it
would be for Flo Jo or Usain Bolt
We try anyways
As we wait
And wait
And clench our jaws

Ball our fists
and direct our eyes
We focus on the goals we can't see
but dream of touching

We wait
And wait
And wait until we can't anymore
like can you come on!
And as fear creeps
While terror tries it's very best to settle in the
stomach
And never does
The gun pops.
Then there's no more waiting.

Hopeless Romantics

Do hopeless romantics ever find what they're
searching for?
Do they ever get the moments they're searching
for in movies?
The coincidental fate
The well thought out first date?
Or are they forced to endure the opposite?
And why?
Why am I on punishment?
For trusting a fantasy?
For imagining that for my entire life I would
eventually find the good in something?
But anyways

Back to the hopeless romantics
Who truly end up hopeless
Truly end up hating love
For all that it does
For all the ways it can bend and break you
Yet when it re-introduces itself to you
You think that maybe this is it

Try to attempt to be an optimist
Just as bluntly as the end of this poem
As soon as you let love back in
It all goes to shit

Beauty in Shades

Always wanted a man whose skin glowed in the
dark like mine
Mixed and created a new shade of melanated love
Out of this world
Larger than all of the galaxies
But as simple as the use of water
As gentle as summer winds
That remains as crisp as the air in autumn
and most of all
The most important of all
I want my love to be unapologetically Black as
The night sky
Black enough to highlight all of its beauty like the
stars in the sky

Over-Commitment

1
I move as 1
Like how the sun gives the moon no directions as
to when it needs to start doing its job
I stand in the night alone
And watch how all the stars shine on their own
But collectively are observed as a whole
I am that.
Many things
A master of none but
The only joker in the deck of all numbers.
I think as two
As you and I
But mostly you
How you think
What you do
How you look at me
That makes me lonely sometimes
As only 1

So I make myself 3
The artist
The athlete
The complicated being
So many things to be involved in
How could I ever feel alone?
I could never feel like the only one in a room
So I observe through 4
4 eyes to watch how earth moves around me
How day turns to night
How energy turns into deprivation
How satisfied turns into starving
How bored turns into busy
And running
And running
And never stopping
And becoming a blur as I spread my soul across
and suddenly contract back into a rubber band
That snaps and is no longer 1
but indeed nothing.

Lonely Comfort

There is a specific comfort that accompanies
being alone
It feels like it's normal when I
want to go to bed naked
or watch a random episode of Friends because I
can't sleep at 5 am

It's okay to laugh in public a little too loud
dance a little too often
Mean mug the world a little too much
It feels nice to speak unapologetically
Because no one is at risk
No feelings have to be spared

A very selfish idea
So selfish at times
I'm concerned I like it too much
Too comfortable with sleeping alone as I toss and
turn in a bed that never really has enough room
for two anyways…

I'm ranting
I do that when I'm alone
and I like it because you don't always
understand it
or me
and I was never really asking you to.

Red, White, and Blood
(disbelief in safe space)

I'll start by saying beliefs change
As tragedies happen and trauma ensues
I find that no space is every truly safe
Unless you're alone
And even that comes with the evils of the mind
The self doubt
And self harm that accompanies it
But that's not today's subject

No space is safe
and it's okay
It's okay to be challenged
To feel attacked
Okay maybe not attacked

But I should feel okay to admit mistakes
I should feel okay to not sensor and hyper-analyze

Every
Single
Thought
As if I'm a damn biochemist for speech
Doesn't add up right?
I know.

And this is not to dismiss the ignorance of others
or the ignorance of myself
but to indeed say
It's okay to not always feel safe
Our parents can not indefinitely hold our hand
We have to decide when it's okay to cross the street
We must look both ways to make sure that WE are good

Do you recognize the emphasis?

When I first realized it, I was upset too
It's a battle of acceptance
To live in any Black body is a battle of something
And this time larger society won
And much as I would love to always feel comfort
I'm not a germaphobe
And I damn sure don't need a plastic bubble

So relax
and challenge yourself to find comfort in the discomfort
Pick another battle to win
Because this one gets us nowhere
With the ignorant still ignorant
And the attacked still feel like victims.

Adaption

All of my dreams have been weird movie scenes
Mashed together from all genres
Just to not make any sense
Sort of like my reality
It's becoming difficult to split them both
Fact and fiction
Into two
But I'm trying to
Trying to understand what's happening
As the past attempts to become present
Prevalent
Relevant
I simply cannot accept it

Is this me we're talking about ?
The same one who talks a good game but is too
shy to speak
oh the irony

Who am I ?
Changing shades like a chameleon
Not with the intention of blending in
But with the purpose of showing all my stripes
Showing all my flaws
Faux-wisdom and all

I am in awe
As I question again, who am I?
Well it depends on who you're asking.
Quite honestly I'm not sure who to even ask.

PERSONAL NARRATIVES OF MY ANXIETY [AND OTHER ISSUES I HAVE]

The Anxiety Series

I'm anxious
To put this pen to paper
and talk about my bad habits
Normalize them through art and call it
creativity

I'm nervous
To acknowledge feelings of any sort
That tip toe to vulnerability
Because you show none
and I fail to have a poker face

I'm jumpy
Thinking every time I check my phone
It'll be _____
But it isn't
and there's some relief in not having to be jumpy
about you
But that's how I am
and I haven't gotten to change it yet
Haven't got the chemical balance quite right
So every night
I think maybe tomorrow
I won't feel so uptight

But still I'm neurotic
Because my skin isn't perfect
And I don't have this life s**t figured out
And I'm tired all the d**n time

And I'm trying to stop cursing in poetry
But how else do I convey ANY EMOTION THAT
FEELS LIKE AN UNENDING RIPPING OF MY
CHEST
Because I've been taught to be anxious.
It's not you, it's me
Quite literally

I'm fearful that I can't fix it
Frightened that I can't tell you
My highly strung
Over sensitive
Deeply embarrassing
Secret.

A Love Letter to
my ANXIETY

I've found life in you
The way you wake me up with my heart trying so
hard to leave my chest
The way you force me to remember to breathe
The way you remind me to listen to podcasts
and listen to music
and dance
and laugh
and pray
All in the company of my own space

I open the blinds and burn herbs
Just in case negative energy is on the way
I pick out my outfit
it's usually sweats everyday
But we putting effort in now because the sun
is out
And seasonal depression is like the snow
Melting away

You make me feel alive
Even in the worst ways
Enhancing every emotion
Especially on my worst days
Forcing me to find perfection in my flaws
and asking them to stay
One day I'll get rid of you
But for now I fight for happiness in all these ways

How the f*ck do I balance my feelings?

I'm attempting many things at once
Multitasking as much as the eight percent of all
my lobes can comprehend
Comprehending how you affirm others
Without sounding like you stole a script from your
favorite rom com
How do I appreciate others without
overwhelming?
How can I confront others, but chill on being
overbearing?
Freaking out
Revealing the scariest part of myself
The biggest secret that even I didn't always know

And sometimes I wish I never did

But here we are
Staring at the results and science doesn't lie
Yet humanity constantly does
Which amplifies this papers truth

And I bet you're wondering what it reads

It says

I will never tell you who I really am because I'm
afraid
Of everything
Of you and your effect
Of me and my reaction

Of the world and all of its uncontrollable factors

So did you decipher the code yet?
figure out what's the real mystery?
Because I haven't
Even though it's hidden in plain sight
Right in front of me

That could be the ignorance talking
They did say it was blissful... whoever that was...

Does it even matter
Do I matter
Do results matter?

Either way
Without the paper
I still have a hamster wheel of a brain
A mess of an equilibrium
A guarded secret locked in the vault

And yes, I threw away the key so I guess I'll never
know how to give affirmations to you or me.

Prelude to an
Anxiety Attack

Darkness and a soft Himalayan pink light fills the
empty space
Thoughts of tomorrow tumble through the air
I broke time purposefully so I don't leave time to
think.
Suddenly my mind rolls the dice and lands on you
The numbers equal out to 5 and 2
The perfect combination for my anxiety
As the memories spark I feel flames engulfing my
conscious
My eyes snap shut to ignore the brightness of your
pain or lack thereof
Smoke fills my nose
my heart attempts to escape from my chest
and for thirty minutes I swallow smoke to accept
the pain you've caused
I ponder on when i will choose to forget you
I wonder if the lies I heard you tell are true
If I'm really that girl
If my love wasn't enough or good enough for your
attention
If you'll go back and make sure I feel like I wasn't
worth your apology
And then the phone rings.

Sentenced to Exile

Another thing to blame
Just lay it all on me, it's not like I'm allowed to
have shame
Standing on trial but it seems the jury already
finds me guilty
"Guilty"!
They yell on multiple counts of loving and doing
your best or improving yourself.
How dare you!
How dare you step outside your comfort zone.
How dare you become vulnerable, you should be
ashamed
and now for your continuous crimes
the penalty is being stuck in it.
I curse you with a broken heart and it's soon to
come
I set the clock and now you are a ticking time
bomb
So what do I do while I'm squared away
In this box, I feel lonely without your embrace
I prepare my statement and it says:
But it's only because your making me feel
that way
I'd climb to the highest mountain for you and yet
you would barely climb a hill
throwing myself out on a limb, but you only let
the bones break
In conclusion, I take my sentence hopefully I will
be able to handle the heartbreak

Shipped off in my shackles, I only hope you were
with me in this confined prison so I wouldn't feel
so lonely.

Nite-mare on my street

I think I'm a monster either way
I'm curious as to why my opinions on this often sway
Because on one hand... I don't know myself
The part I knew is changing and I can't call out for
help
Something claws for a way out
A hunger roars to be fed
I'm stuck in my own lions den
But I like it there sometimes
The evil in my eyes and the twist in my lips is
appealing to me
The perceived notion that I am insane
precedes me
and maybe I am
Maybe my monster is loud and inhumane
Maybe it's a terror I'm not looking to tame
But on the other hand
I'm a horror because you've told me I am

Raging insecurities turn into bitching tendencies
I can't tell when I'm right or wrong
Justification doesn't seem moral and neither do I
When did it become so easy for me to lie
So splendid to not feel
So easy to not feel real
I am a being
or am I a beast?
I lay naked in the woods lost and confused
but ready to eat

Bad at Healthy Arguing

I wish I was less considerate with my words
I wish I never bit my tongue because when you
left, it was gushing blood from the knife you stuck
in it
The whiteness of my teeth lost its cleanliness
As anger ripped through my voice and tore you to
shreds
But only in my mind
Outside I was silent
The warm air beat me to the punch in my
stomach
My lungs lost all feeling
Lost all knowledge on how to produce sound
I could only produce pain
You only produce pain
It was your gift to me as Eve gave Adam the fruit
You placed it in a golden plate with soft sweet
words as the side
And my gullible heart ate it
Also wallowed the shards of metal you hid

The blades cut my throats and I hated it
But I loved you, so I never went to first aid
Never got the band aid
Never cleaned the wound
So the iron in my blood rusts as the love I had for
you turns into a disgraceful brown that represents
the way you left my heart
Dying.

Generational Curses

A familiar fingerprint is drowned in the blood of
our genetics
I see that the mark will leave its impression on
you too
I wished it wouldn't
I wished the best for you
All the happiness and normalcy in morality I
never got to see
But in a deck full of stacked cards, you got it the
worst

Bottled In

People get selfish at funerals
Think about how this person affected their life
How pain rests in their heart at night
I do something worse
I get mad for no reason
and you would never know it
Just how you would never know that the person in
the casket had last thoughts
Just like how my body is a literal coke bottle and if
you shake me hard enough
I'll burst
I will fizzle and pop into no existence
I will become
A waste
The casket will close
My anger will be the death of me
Or will it be my unconscious acceptance of not
knowing me?
Not knowing my own thoughts

Focusing too much on the person who lays in the
casket
Who never cared about me

Who I loved so hard anyways
Who I tried to help always
Because I mentally cannot help it
Physically cannot control when my face skews
into a concerned frown that turns upside down
into a sympathetic smile with a hug on the side
That gives you all the help you could ask for and
all the advice you'll choose to ignore
My desert runs dry with innocent sweet smiles
But every once in a while the oasis refills itself
with the need to fix you
So watch out
I'll fix you so much that I break you
Give you holes where you didn't know they could
create themselves
While you patch yourself up with duct tape, I'll
fester those holes into gaping spaces
That suck me into universes that God created but
unknowingly began to revolve around you
So eventually I'll have to make you the man in the
casket
That way I can close it and forget your universe
ever existed.

6 Degrees

My mind likes to play tricks on itself
My heart likes to tie my stomach in knots for fun
and watch me solve it like a rubix cube
Stress knows me the best because I be pressed
About everything
I'm trying to separate the fact from the imaginary
the way they do in libraries
But let's face it, my dewey decimal system has
been all out of order for quite some time
Trying to separate family business from my big
mouth
Trying to separate temporary flutters of emotions
from prolonged seasons of feelings
I
Just
Can't
Process
Enough
I wish my mind could be like the planners I
write in

Check off all the boxes and make sure everything
fit in them but instead I can't even get the key to
get them out of storage
So they just sit
Grow some mold and the useful items I once held
The facts I once knew
Eventually waste away
I don't want to waste away
I'm trying to know me but I'm so damn
complicated that I am
So
Tired of getting as deep as the ocean with myself
I am drowning in my own sea of confusing ass
concepts that are supposed to explain why my
heart keeps beating in my chest and dropping to
my stomach and picking up its heart rate all at the
same damn time
I'm nervous
That I'll lose everyone else
Just to find myself.

Blindside and its spots

I've always been a sucker for uncertain men
men with death wishes
They were always more passionate anyways
You put fear in me
You shoved it down my throat without choice at
times when the moon is high
Making me generate endless reasons why no one
will ever love me like you did
But you never did
You just leave false impressions by creating a
house of mirrors and pointing all the blame at me
Suddenly, I believe it
So congrats
Please come accept your award for breaking me
just the right way
Even I didn't see it coming
You left my vase with a crack in it
Making it to where I'll never be bought again
Never put on display to be shown off

You made it bad enough to where I reminisce of
you, but still feel guilty enough when you look at
me in disgust
I hope you're proud that I fight the demons you
could never face

Anxiety Trait: Conforming

Life is a bubble that I'm trying to coexist in
But y'all are taking up the air
My lungs are praying for help
To be relieved of their burden of over working
themselves
I've been overworking myself
Trying to please you and you and you
And I've left nothing for me
I feel nothing for me
As I go days almost weeks and don't eat
Nothing sounds good I say
And my favorites go to waste as I waste away
Why am I wasting away?
Because none of you cared anyways
Didn't care that I toss and turn and take Benadryl
as I yearn for rest
To close my eyes and actually drift away
Instead my nightmares snatch my soul and leave
my body stuck in a trance as my eyes

Dance across the ceiling and try to catch up with
the moonlight
The sun is too bright and the clouds are too dark
I don't even know where my days start
But they end with me crying and hearing my
stomach rumble as I know it sheds a few more
pounds and my self esteem crumbles
And I ask myself,
Why am I wasting away?
Are you doing this to me?
Or am I punishing myself for being a contributor
to living in the pain only I can see?

Lessons from Aretha

Aretha Franklin got it right when she literally
spelled it out for us
How hard is it to respect me?
As I've watched you respect him and her
especially ya momma
and her momma
and even that girl you really liked when we
first met
Is it something I said?
A vibe I sent because i've been working for 20
years
Been stepped on by many
Seen by a few
So if you're gonna choose to do this…
Who am I kidding?
I can't promise consequences
My heart is soft for whoever shows an atom of
affection
It forgives without a second of consideration for
self
It actually uses "it's okay" as a popular phrase
and never says no
Never yells
or bickers

Let's avoid fighting for now because when I let loose
The hurricane of hurtful words rolls in with a tide so
high you'll drown
Then I can't save you
But it isn't my job to be a lifeguard
Knowing me I'd still try to drain the water out of
your lungs
I won't even protect myself
I'll leave myself exposed and let the tide drag me
out into an abyss
I'll let you drag me to the bottom
Use me like a mule because I just need some
affection
But we've heard that a million times
Heard how lonely it gets
How you're the last hope, knowing you're one of
many
How I don't know how these feelings will fade,
but give me a day
Okay maybe a month
If we're keeping it honest
Because I refuse to go to bed crying
While you slept peacefully
Undisturbed
Disrespecting me like it's as easy as counting sheep

A Midnight Spiral

I dream until I can't
As pessimism draws me from slumber
Pulls its best men to the forefront
and aims for my ego like no one ever could
There's no need to attempt a surprise attack on me
My army is self destructive
It faces an issue with corruption like no other
Spinning webs of doubt
Throwing needles of positivity in the haystack
Down to eventually fall out and never be found
What's the point of being poked anyways
a painful reminder to live
Instead I'll take the numbness of feeling worthless
as syrup slides down my throat
Coating it in thoughts of your true thoughts of me
Thoughts hypothesized
Socially experimented upon by daily activities of
asking for someone to talk to me
Am I worth talking to?
What's so interesting?
No not that .. that's just weird
Analyzing why
Because I've never been popular anyways
Shit I thought lame kids were in now anyways
But being the trend avoided I am
I am just another lost in the shadows

Coming to the conclusion that my name will
Never be good enough for 20, 15, 10, or none
I knock my hypothesis of being accepted
and now I'm back to square one.

An Undiagnosed Addiction

Sometimes
A click
Double tap
Wandering eyes
On an app
Is all I have

Instagram paints all my pictures and plays all my
favorite things as I watch life go without me
As my friends find love
or at least a man who finds them pretty
As he gets his first car for his 21st birthday
As she travels to Greece for a post grad trip
What you don't get to see is most important
pay attention
As I double tap I search for happiness
As I watch myself reflect in the screen laying in a
twin sized bed
With a canopy
A canopy with the straightest of faces
and the deadest eyes
Like I'm a queen or something
I am the queen of dry deserts and no notifications
as I tap on Twitter to get in my average amount of
laughs for the day
As I relate to everyone
sharing childhood memories

Sharing our hidden secrets hoping someone
Double taps for relation
Sharing pain in the safety of night mode
Sharing gross opinions about school shootings that
everyone chooses to advocate for
How about we retweet it?
That will get awareness for sure!
I'm so fucking tired of retweeting
so I don't
I don't feel when another student dies
or a Black boy is shot on T.V.
Because I can't do anything
So I scroll past it with annoyance as everyone
offers thoughts and prayers
The world has too many problems for me to pray for

I'm a horrible person
maybe that's why I use Snapchat filters
To fill in the cracks of my flaws
To cover up the red eyes and bruised lungs from
when I was screaming for help
I'm so sad
Maybe because when no one responds to me I
know they had something better to do
Something is wrong with me
because I go all day and I won't hear from a soul
Is it just me?
That's the answer that double tapping a screen
won't give me.

Today
I almost deleted all of my apps
Until I realized
That was all that I had.

Feeling Sorry For Myself and Fatherless Figures

All the men who have ever entered my life have
broken me
Upon mention of a name there is a thrust of pain
that takes a little bit of my life away
But I still let you enter in anyways
Because you are all I got
Because I can't help but love
I can't help but know i'll be broken anyways
So I might as well be able to pick and choose who
does it
I might as well be able to cast the role for my
series
The plot twist is I'll never stop loving
Never stop sharing stories of pain hoping to find
relief and I never do
I never feel valued or cherished or deemed
worthy enough of a normal man in my life
I pray for normal men in my life
As my past preys on me

Dealing with Diagnosis

I am absolutely furious and hurt and disgusted
At how my friendship means so little
I can't open up
I just take it
Take all the judgment because it has to be me
every single time

I'm so sad
That nobody hears me
As I cry myself to sleep
To escape the sorrow that life brings
Would you believe me if I told you how lonely I
felt inside?
How it's met by a yearning for some sort of love
that I can't seem to afford
I guess only the good can receive good things.

Discomfort That Leads to Anxiety Attacks

I hate rooms where I don't feel comfortable
The space is too open
Eyes wander like cameras
Ears listen to pick up waves like mics
and unfamiliar bodies fill the space
Fill me with this feeling that if I don't rip myself
out of this skin I'll never fit in

But since I am not like the characters Ovid has
written
I lack the ability to metamorph into anything but a
wallflower who tries to fly on the wall unnoticed

I'm very careful with my spaces
So how dare you intrude with arrogance and
narcissism
It's so large I hope you see yourself in a river and
drown in it
Or you can just leave
Or we both know I'm so awkward
So anxiety attack bound
So likely to trip over a surface on the way out
So I'll go.
I'll find a new space outside where the air is limitless
Where it's impossible for me to count the things I
don't like bout you
So I count the stars instead

An attacking poem

While panic hits the fan   In
I search for a window   Out
Scan for oxygen, but find no recollection of it in   In
my lungs   Out
I trace the halls with my anxiety   Think
Deers caught in the headlights are nothing   Stop
compared to the blank slate that becomes my face   You
I am gone   Are
I am   Okay
Focused on everything outside of the scope   But am I?
As panic hits the fan
I think of you hitting me
The dreadful fantasy of feeling your grip in the
wrong way when I least expect it
Preying on me like a lion prowling towards a
gazelle
My legs can't travel fast enough
but my eyes can as I find a window
My clams hold no pearls so why can't I grip this
fucking window handle ?!

5 minutes later

Cold wind sweeps up the panic like grandma's
porch and sprinkles of revelation force me back
Pound me back to life with the constant repeat of

Overthinking

I think I'm so emotional because of my birth control

I think I'm so lit because I'm using music to
express joy from my repressed body

I think I'm so thoughtful outside of the classroom
because my brain isn't forced to think within four
walls

Able to stretch past the space in between the lines
and can rearrange words in ways I've never seen

I think I'm tired of love because I always fail at it

I think I'm good at choosing men who turn out to
be problematic

I think I'm too much for other people

I think I'm too little for success

All I want is to stop thinking and be able to
actually rest

The Pessoptimist Imbalance

Why do we celebrate birthdays?
As bones break and bills pile up
Life gets harder in every way
Trials and tribulations become cyclical
I just don't want to be sick anymore
So that when my birthday comes
I can celebrate
All-day
The full 24 hours
See it's always been the other way
Another disappointment
Constant reminders
This is your day
Don't ruin your day
Why do you make it about anyone else anyway?
Because that's how I live all the other 364 days

When I Got Really
Tired of Poetry

Do you wanna know what I loathe about being me
The part I hate to admit
Imagine this:
A continuous bike ride I'm always on
The sky is gray
The land is foggy, reflecting my thought process
Never stopping for hydration or fuel
Just a perpetual cycle
That loves, breaks, writes, repeats
and the wheels keep spinning
I have written poems about 2 things
Love and my disfunction
I have created muses out of bodies that don't want
to be painted
But purely have no choice as I watch like the feds
And create art as slyly as a fox
Hang it up in my soul so that it can finally get
some fresh air and dry
But it'll continue to get dirty
Continue to find some sort of way to lose its color

You see all of these feelings could never fit in a box
Only lines
Only into words that paint pretty pictures and
murderous thunderstorms

Only into pages that scream for me to fill them
with more
Pain
Rage
Heartbreak
Happiness
Lust
Wonder
Pause
What do I do when all the pages are filled with
the same content?
Writing the same script over and over
releasing the same serial of soaps based on Korri's
sad ass excuse of a love life
I wish I had written about more than my first two
heartbreaks
about more than how my daddy left me
about more than seasonal depression
More than everything!
I want everything
I want to feel more
breathe more
see more
Please let me be more than a faux da Vinci who
can't let go of his Mona Lisa

Zoloft Candy

So tired of popping pills
Makes me feel like a drug addict
Addicted to the feeling of being happy
More like addicted to the feeling of feeling alive
But not the alive I've been lately

Lately, it's been random crying
For hours
The way it can't stop
And part of me doesn't want it to
Or the way I can't sleep so I lay here
Feeling exhaustion like an overworked teacher
Teaching you to feel what I feel
Anyways

ARM DAY

There are days like this
When misery hangs onto me like clothes in the
closet
Where tears hold back
Where anger festers
And I reach for help
Reach for something
And I'm left empty handed
Heart empty handed
Lungs out of air
Bench pressing depression for fun
And I have no rack
So it sits on my chest
Waiting for me to accept defeat

If I Could Sew Myself

I clean my wounds
Thinking that stops the bleeding
I stitch them up
But the knots won't stay in place for long
Leaving gaping holes and scars
My healing methods aren't up to par
If sleep is a cousin of death, then time must be a
disease
I keep trying to save me from me
But no matter how many times i stitch the wound
The thread just keeps slipping.

Dogs Smell Fear (Paranoia)

I sit in my fear constantly

As I sit and wait for responses, but I get messages
from nobody

I guess they wouldn't know

They aren't dogs

in the way they smell fear at least

And I reek of it

You can smell my deepest worries like it was a
fragrance

I swear people just do their best to not breathe it in

Yet sometimes I get told I smell good

If only they knew the work that I put in to scrub
the scent away

I let the water drown out my tears and let the
steam sweat it out of my pores

But there's always something left

As a new day comes there isn't enough time to
breathe slow breaths

There isn't enough time for a nap

Silent spaces are always still too big

So I curl up in my bed

Being held by my insecurities and anxiety

Waiting for someone, anyone to pick up the scent

Suicidal Ideations

Who am I too much for?
I just need to release all the evil things in my mind
Cleanse the demon like thoughts that cross my
tongue
Can I tell you all of them?
Can you handle it?
Or will you jump at the sound of death that leaves
my lips
Run and hide
Leave me alone
in my depths of despair
My pool of tears
My bed of nervousness
As I cry out for help
knowing nobody can hear me.

Melatonin Nights (When Insomnia Started)

As others cuddle up to their lovers
I cuddle up to my melatonin
A sleeping aid for some, a memory reliever for me
Covering up the fact that the cold is only nice with
your arms wrapped around me
And the warmth is only welcoming with the heat
of our bodies
But that option ceases to exist.
So I look for something else
How long will it take until I need something
stronger than melatonin?

The Time my Anxiety Cost me 15lbs

I've been in fear of form fitting dresses for
months now
Can you still see my ribs through them?
Everyone swears it's my ab's
But I can't get past that gut feeling that my gut is
getting smaller and everyone can see
Everyone can tell
Tell that I'm unhealthy
No no no
Not physically, mentally
The weight I had
It was good
It was beautiful
I carried it well
Felt well in it
Felt warm like I didn't need hugs from no man
Felt like summer days and endless meals
Felt like sweat well deserved and well placed
But now I don't feel that I inhabit that same space

Only a shell is left
and I feel homeless
Displaced out of my own shape
Craving to get it back
But knowing the way to get there sets me back in
other ways
No longer the record breaker

No longer the athlete
Just some thick girl
Who catches attention when she walks down the
street
Am I wrong?
For craving attention in that way?
For wanting to feel beautiful in my own way?

I can tell it's why I'm not wanted
Overlooked
Not considered the category of bad bitches
but instead
I'm one of the homies
Oh, what an honor to have all of my sex appeal
sucked away the moment you get past my face
and see my nonexistent waist

I wish I could say it gets better when I strip the
clothes away...
But as you do, I fold my arms across my chest and
attempt to hide everything from you
Because for now I feel too small for the frame
Too fragile
Like I might break
But I've already been broken
So I guess there's no frame for me to fit in anyways.

Trying New Sleep Meds

I use you whenever I need you
Which is every night
Every time like clockwork
A slip two out of the bottle
Wishing they were peppermints
As I swallow them dry
and then I wait
Twiddle my thumbs
Or twist my hair
Watch my shows and think of how life is so unfair
That some people get to naturally fall asleep
As for me
I see double after thirty minutes
as my eyes try to focus on the tv screen
and slowly
I
    Dri
         Ft
Away

from the night and effortlessly slip into the sun
greeting me for another day

Tired of Anxiety and Other Things

Will I ever get a chance to make a decision
Without having my rib cage laced up like new
sneakers?
Give my lungs a chance to use themselves
To not have my heart beat like a hummingbird
pecks
Just to be able to slow things down
always speeding things up
Maybe it's the athlete in me
You know the one that jumps at the whistle
Shoots out of the blocks as the gun goes off
Imagine the moment when you jump in the pool
Realize it's too cold
Urge to get out
Act like it never happened
But it did

So here we are
Guessing that maybe it's from the trauma of
childhood
Not too traumatic.
Nothing horrific
Just blacking out from abuse or crying from self
hate
Self hate that comes from competitions you didn't
start and daddy issues that pile up like child
support

Maybe it's from the threats you never heard
just felt
Or the scars you saw but never knew how they
got there
Maybe it's unknown
Maybe it's biological
Scientifically unchangeable
Built in just like the nervous system
Maybe it's unnatural like we try to make cancer
sound
Even though it's in ya from the day we're born
Just deactivated
Until one day
You have a reason to fear everything
So you do
Fear intimacy as much as you fear death
and fear success just as much as you fear failure
Then again... I don't know anything
but self doubt is a whole other issue.

Balancing Act

I teeter between being okay and feeling like the
world is on fire every thirty seconds
Which means half of every minute
I am afraid
anxious
nervous
The living embodiment of sweaty palms and
shaking nerves
But inside feels like that too
Inside doesn't feel like butterflies
But instead the home for caterpillars to nest and
grow inside of me
Ew
Another visual please
My anxiety acts so quickly
I might become terrified of small worms who
mean no harm
Neither do my meds
But here we are

Contemplating what I should do if the world were
to catch on fire
right this very second
Even though it is snowing
I will profess my love to all 12 of my soulmates
Yes it has to be an even number
And I'm currently at 11